70 YEARS OF POPULAR MUSIC

THE·EIGHTIES
PART TWO

D1147123

Edited by PETER FOSS

WARNER BROS/IMP

First published 1988 © International Music Publications
Exclusive Distributors: International Music Publications, Southend Road, Woodford Green, Essex IG8 8HN, England
252-2-28, Order Ref: 16966, ISBN 0 8635 570 7

ALWAYS ON MY MIND

Words and Music by WAYNE THOMPSON,
MARK JAMES and JOHN CHRISTOPHER

VERSE 2:
Maybe I didn't hold you all those lonely, lonely times.
And I guess I never told you I'm so happy that you're mine.
If I made you feel second best, I'm so sorry. I was blind.

(CHORUS)

A BOY FROM NOWHERE

Words and Music by
M LEANDER and E SEAGO

8

AXEL F

By HAROLD FALTERMEYER

Moderately fast, with a strong beat ♩ = 126

N.C.

12

BAD

Words and Music
by MICHAEL JACKSON

Medium Dance Groove

No Chord

Your

N.C.

butt is mine,   gon - na tell you right.   Just
giv - ing you   on count of three   to

* These chords contain no 3rds.

4

*Sing the lyrics between the asterisks 2nd time only.

Additional Lyrics
(For repeat)

You know I'm smooth-I'm
bad-you know it
(Bad bad-really, really bad)
You know I'm bad-I'm
bad baby
(Bad bad-really, really bad)
You know, you know, you
know it-come on
(Bad bad-really, really bad)
And the whole world has to
answer right now
(And the whole world has to
answer right now)
Woo!
(Just to tell you once again)

You know I'm bad, I'm bad-
you know it
(Bad bad-really, really bad)
You know I'm bad-you know-hoo!
(Bad bad-really, really bad)
You know I'm bad-I'm bad-
you know it, you know
(Bad bad-really, really bad)
And the whole world has to
answer right now
(And the whole world has to
answer right now)
Just to tell you once again...
(Just to tell you once
again...)
Who's bad?

BECAUSE OF YOU

Words and Music by KEVIN ROWLAND,
HELEN O'HARA and BILLY ADAMS

And if   you need some place to   be _____   You're al - right   with

BIG LOVE

Words and Music
by LINDSEY BUCKINGHAM

Oh, I'll build _____ you a king - dom in that
Oh, you begged _____ me to keep you in that

house _____ on the hill. ——
house _____ on the hill. ——

Look-ing out for love, _____

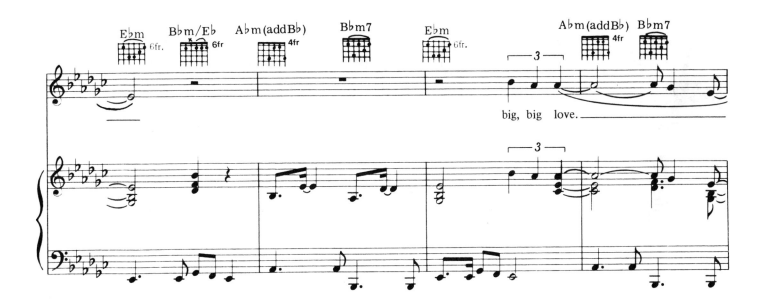

big, big love. _____

28

big,   big   love.

3rd Verse

I wake up
alone with it all.
I wake up
but only to fall.

CAN'T BE WITH YOU TONIGHT

Words and Music
by F L DA SILVA

COMING AROUND AGAIN

Words and Music
by CARLY SIMON

37

CHINA IN YOUR HAND

Words and Music by
CAROL DECKER and RON ROGERS

CRAZY FOR YOU

Words and Music by
JON LIND and JOHN BETTIS

44

GOT MY MIND SET ON YOU

Words and Music
by RUDY CLARK

IF YOU LET ME STAY

Words and Music
by TERENCE TRENT D'ARBY

(CHORUS)

If you let me stay _____ I'll say what I should - 've said
But if you let me

if you let me stay _____ I should have said that I ____ love you

if you let me stay _____ And I should have said it from _ my heart

if you let me stay _____ 'cos I need ya I'm not a man with-out you ba -

EVERYWHERE

Words and Music
by CHRISTINE McVIE

3rd Verse

Can you hear me calling
out you name?
You know that I'm falling
and I don't know what to say.

Come along baby
We better make a start.
You better make it soon
before you break my heart.

I JUST CALLED TO SAY I LOVE YOU

Words and Music
by STEVIE WONDER

I GET WEAK

Words and Music
by DIANE WARREN

LA ISLA BONITA

Words and Music by MADONNA CICCONE,
PAT LEONARD and BRUCE GAITSCH

Last night I dreamt of San Pe - dro,
I fell in love with San Pe - dro,
girl. (Instrumental)

LIKE A VIRGIN

Words and Music by
BILLY STEINBERG and TOM KELLY

L A LAW

By MIKE POST

84

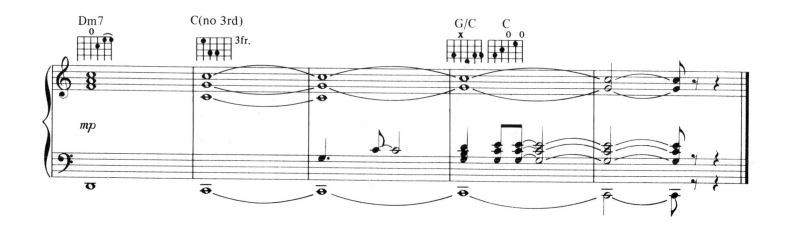

LITTLE LIES

Words and Music
by CHRISTINE McVIE and EDDY QUINTELA

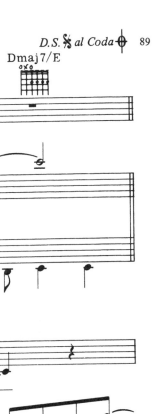

Repeat and fade

Coda

Tell me lies,____ tell me sweet lit-tle lies.____

(Tell me lies.) ____
(Tell me, tell me lies.)

Oh no,____ no____ you

can't dis-guise.____

*(You can't dis - guise.)*____
(No you can't dis-guise.)

LOVE LETTERS

Words by EDWARD HEYMAN
Music by VICTOR YOUNG

THE LOOK OF LOVE

Words and Music by
MADONNA CICCONE and PAT LEONARD

NEVER GONNA GIVE YOU UP

Words and Music by
STOCK, AITKEN and WATERMAN

NIKITA

Words and Music by
ELTON JOHN and BERNIE TAUPIN

Hey Nik - it - a is it cold___ In your lit - tle corn - er
Do you ev - er dream of me,___ Do you ev - er see the let - ters

of the world? You could roll a - round the globe
that I write? When you look up through the wire,

no, Nik-it - a___you'll nev-er___ know.

NOTHING'S GONNA STOP US NOW

Words and Music by
ALBERT HAMMOND and DIANE WARREN

PART-TIME LOVER

Words and Music
by STEVIE WONDER

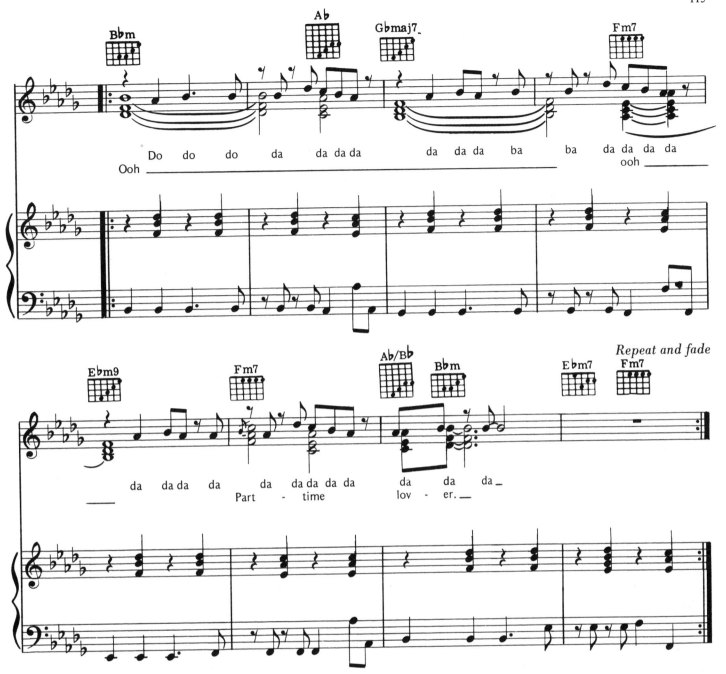

Verse 3:

I've got something that I must tell;
Last night someone rang our doorbell
And it was not you, my part-time lover.

And then a man called our exchange
But didn't want to leave his name,
I guess that two can play the game of *(To Coda:)*

RUNNING UP THAT HILL

Words and Music
by KATE BUSH

118

SAVING ALL MY LOVE FOR YOU

Words by GERRY GOFFIN
Music by MICHAEL MASSER

124

SAY YOU, SAY ME

Words and Music
by LIONEL RICHIE

SEPARATE LIVES

Words and Music
by STEPHEN BISHOP

Chorus:

134

REFRAIN 2:

Well, I held on to let you go.
And if you lost your love for me,
You never let it show.
There was no way to compromise.
So now we're living separate lives.

REFRAIN 3:

You have no right to ask me how I feel.
You have no right to speak to me so kind.
Someday I **might** find myself looking in your eyes.
But for now, we'll go on living separate lives.
Yes, for now we'll go on living separate lives.

STARTING TOGETHER

Words and Music
by BILL BUCKLEY

Moderately

We're start-ing to-

geth - er, _____ We're tak-ing a chance _____ on what we

feel. We're start-ing to - geth - er _____ Be-cause we be-lieve _____

_____ our love is real. We'll pro-mise to have and to hold _____ From this day on _____

STAND BY ME

Words and Music by BEN E. KING,
JERRY LEIBER and MIKE STOLLER

142

TAKE MY BREATH AWAY

Words and Music by
GIORGIO MORODER and TOM WHITLOCK

Verse 2:
Watching, I keep waiting, still anticipating love,
Never hesitating to become the fated ones.
Turning and returning to some secret place to hide;
Watching in slow motion as you turn my way and say,
"Take my breath away." *(To Bridge:)*

Verse 3:
Watching every motion in this foolish lover's game;
Haunted by the notion somewhere's there's a love in flames.
Turning and returning to some secret place inside;
Watching in slow motion as you turn to me and say,
"Take my breath away." *(To Coda:)*

TELL IT TO MY HEART

Words and Music by
ERNIE GOLD and SETH SWIRSKY

on - ly one, is this real - ly love or just a game. _____ Tell it to my

heart, I can feel my bo - dy rock, ev - 'ry time you call ___ my name.

THAT'S THE WAY IT IS

Words and Music by
STOCK, AITKEN and WATERMAN

THAT'S WHAT FRIENDS ARE FOR

Words and Music by
CAROLE BAYER SAGER and BURT BACHARACH

TOGETHER FOREVER

Words and Music by
STOCK, AITKEN and WATERMAN

If there's an-y-thing you need ___ all you have to do is say ___
If they ev-er get ___ you down ___ there's al-ways some-thing I can do ___

geth-er for-ev-er with __ you. ___ (%) To- geth-er for-ev- er with __

you. ___

D.S. and Repeat Chorus to Fade

So

TRUE COLORS

Words and Music by
BILLY STEINBERG and TOM KELLY

WEAK IN THE PRESENCE OF BEAUTY

Words and Music by
MICHAEL WARD and ROB CLARKE

WHENEVER YOU NEED SOMEBODY

Words and Music by
STOCK, AITKEN and WATERMAN

much too late for you ___ to change your ways ___ I
you will nev-er know ___ just how good ___ I feel ___ the
much too late for you ___ to change your ways ___ I

can't ___ keep ___ hold-ing on ___ ex - pect - ing you to stay. ___
joy ___ in - side of me ___ makes me feel so real. ___
can't ___ keep ___ hold-ing on ___ ex - pect - ing you to stay. ___

When you're all a-lone and if ___ you're feel-ing down ___ call ___ me I'll be a - round. ___

YOU WIN AGAIN

Words and Music by BARRY GIBB,
ROBIN GIBB and MAURICE GIBB

175

Printed in Great Britain by
St Edmundsbury Press Limited, Bury St Edmunds, Suffolk   7/88